Doctor Daze and the Bamboozler

by Kay Woodward
Illustrated by Bill Ledger

OXFORD
UNIVERSITY PRESS

In this story ...

Evan
(Flex)

Evan is super stretchy. He can stretch his body in any direction.

Nisha
(Nimbus)

Nisha has the power to control the weather. She can make it sunny or stormy.

"Hurry up, Evan," said Nisha. "I can't wait to get to the Lexis City Gadget Show!"

"It doesn't open for another ten minutes," Evan panted, as he ran after her.

"I want to be first through the doors. I'm so excited, I could make a whirlwind!" said Nisha.

"You can't make a whirlwind here," said Evan, looking around nervously.

"I'm just joking," replied Nisha. "I know the rules. When we're outside the academy, we've got to act like normal children. No one must see us doing anything *super*."

The gadget show was amazing! The huge hall was packed with stands. Evan didn't know where to look first. There were Pocket Jets, Rocket Boots, Hover Umbrellas, and lots of other cool gadgets.

It would have been easy to get lost at the show, but luckily there was a Power Projector showing a map on the wall.

"Where shall we go first?" asked Evan. "How about over there?" Nisha replied.

Evan looked over at a crowd standing around a bright purple stand. There was a sign above it saying: *BAMBOOZLER – ON SALE HERE.*

A tall woman with black, glossy hair was in charge of the stand. She wore dark glasses and was holding something that looked like a telescope. It was super sleek and very shiny.

Evan frowned. The woman seemed familiar.

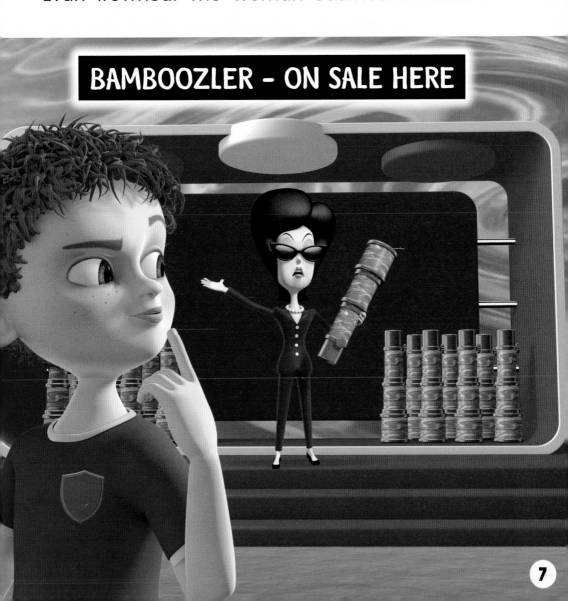

BAMBOOZLER - ON SALE HERE

"What does the Bamboozler do?" asked Evan.

"*Just look and see ...*" the woman chanted softly, holding it out for him to peer through.

"Er, no thanks," said Evan, who had just seen a Supersonic Flying Disc on the next stand.

"Can I have a go?" asked Nisha.

"Of course," said the woman, handing over the shiny gadget. *"Just look and see ..."*

Nisha shut one eye and stared into the Bamboozler with the other.

Evan wandered off to the next stand.

"What have you been doing?" Evan asked Nisha a few minutes later.

"Looking into the Bamboozler," said Nisha, gazing at him blankly.

"Oh," Evan replied. "Well, take a look at this Zillion 3000. It's the fastest drone ever. Awesome!"

"Awesome," said Nisha slowly.

Evan frowned. Nisha seemed a little strange. Perhaps she'd snap out of it if he showed her even more amazing inventions!

It took them all afternoon to look around the show. Evan kept trying to talk to Nisha, but she still seemed to be in a daze.

At closing time, there was a dazzling laser show. Colourful lights flashed and zapped all around.

"Wow," breathed Evan. "Isn't it incredible, Nisha?"

He turned around, but Nisha wasn't listening. Instead she was walking towards the Bamboozler stand.

Evan ran after Nisha. When he saw her face, he gasped. "What's wrong with your eyes?" he asked. They were all colours of the rainbow, and the colours were spinning round and round like the spokes of a bicycle wheel.

Nisha said nothing. She just kept on walking.

Nisha wasn't the only one walking towards the stand. Hundreds of people were heading the same way, their eyes a whirl of colour.

Evan watched in horror. Something was *really* wrong.

The tall woman raised her arms. "I am Doctor Daze. I have bamboozled you with my Bamboozler!" she cried. "Now you will do as I say!"

Evan gasped. Doctor Daze! He knew he had seen her before.

Doctor Daze

Catchphrase: I'll daze you for days!

Hobbies: inventing gadgets.

Likes: people who do what she says, chocolate biscuits.

Dislikes: everyone else in the world!

Beware! Doctor Daze has made a number of gadgets that control people's minds. If you spot her, run the other way!

"Next, I will bamboozle everyone in Lexis City," Doctor Daze continued. "Then I will bamboozle the world. EVERYONE will do as I say!"

Evan gritted his teeth. He was the only one who wasn't bamboozled because he hadn't looked into the Bamboozler. It was up to him to save the day!

Evan thought hard. He *had* to stop Doctor Daze, but how could he do that without revealing his power?

Then Evan glanced around. Everyone was bamboozled! They were all staring at Doctor Daze. No one was looking at him.

Quickly, Evan stretched out one arm to grab the Bamboozler from Doctor Daze. She let out a shriek.

With his other hand, Evan pulled Doctor Daze's dark glasses off. Then, before she could move, he held the Bamboozler up to her face.

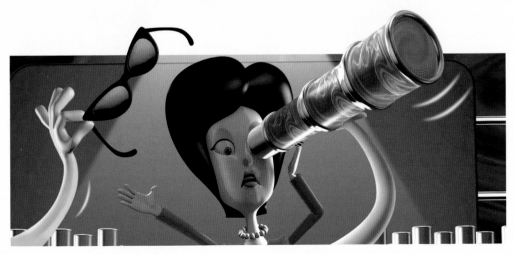

When Evan took the Bamboozler away, Doctor Daze's rainbow eyes whirled round and round.

"DOCTOR DAZE," commanded Evan, "GO TO THE POLICE STATION AND GIVE YOURSELF UP, NOW!"

The bamboozled Doctor Daze headed for the door, mumbling, "Police station. Now."

Evan flipped the Bamboozler around and held it up to Nisha's face so that she was looking through the wrong end. Would it reverse the Bamboozler's effect? Yes! The colours faded from her eyes.

"Evan? What's going on?" asked Nisha.

"I'll explain later," Evan promised.

Evan had a brilliant idea that not even Doctor Daze had thought of.

He grabbed the Power Projector and used it to send an image from the wrong end of the Bamboozler onto the wall.

The bamboozled crowd all stared up at the projection. Within seconds, they were back to normal.

People started to leave the show. They all seemed to have forgotten about the Bamboozler.

As Nisha and Evan were walking back to the academy, Nisha asked, "Are you going to tell me what *really* happened today?"

"I just saved the city from a baddie who wanted to control everyone's minds," said Evan, beaming.

"You did *what*?" said Nisha, looking utterly bamboozled.

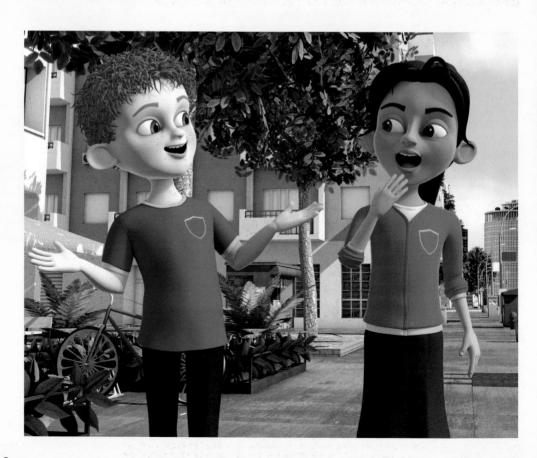